NASCAR RACING

Talladega Superspeedway

by A. R. Schaefer

Consultant:
Suzanne Wise, Librarian
Stock Car Racing Collection, Belk Library
Appalachian State University
Boone, North Carolina

Capstone
press

Mankato, Minnesota

Edge Books are published by Capstone Press,
151 Good Counsel Drive, P.O. Box 669, Mankato, Minnesota 56002.
www.capstonepress.com

Library of Congress Cataloging-in-Publication Data
Schaefer, A. R. (Adam Richard), 1976-
  Talladega superspeedway / by A.R. Schaefer.
  p. cm.—(Edge Books NASCAR racing)
  Includes bibliographical references and index.
  ISBN-13: 978-0-7368-4379-9 (hardcover)
  ISBN-10: 0-7368-4379-5 (hardcover)
  1. Alabama International Motor Speedway—Juvenile literature. 2. Automobile
racing—Alabama—Talladega—Juvenile literature. I. Title. II. Series.
GV1033.5.A42S33 2007
796.7'2068761—dc22   2005037075

Summary: Discusses the track design, history, and exciting races at
    Talladega Superspeedway.

Editorial Credits
Tom Adamson, editor; Jason Knudson, set designer; Patrick D. Dentinger,
    book designer; Jo Miller, photo researcher

Photo Credits
AP Wide World Photos/Jay Sailors, 15; Dave Martin, 22; Dan Lighton, 24, 25; Curtis
    Compton, 28
Getty Images Inc./Streeter Lecka, cover; Donald Miralle, 5, 8; Jamie Squire, 7; Chris
    Stanford, 12; Darrell Ingham, 13; Jonathan Ferrey, 14, 27; Craig Jones, 29
SportsChrome Inc./Rob Tringali, 16
The Sharp Image/Sam Sharpe, 11, 19, 21

1 2 3 4 5 6 11 10 09 08 07 06

Table of Contents

CHAPTER 1

Winner by Inches

Talladega Superspeedway in Alabama gives fans an exciting, tense race. The Aaron's 499 on April 21, 2002, was no different.

Jimmie Johnson started the race from the pole position. Dale Earnhardt Jr. started in fourth position, but he quickly took the lead.

Race cars screamed around the track at more than 190 miles (306 kilometers) per hour. Drivers tried to gain extra speed by drafting. Each driver stayed just inches from the car in front of him. Racing this close is dangerous, but everyone wanted to catch up to race leader Earnhardt. Earnhardt led 133 of the 188 laps.

It didn't take long for Dale Earnhardt Jr. to take the lead in the 2002 Aaron's 499.

Learn about:

→ An exciting race

→ A close finish

→ Talladega basics

With less than 25 laps to go, disaster struck for more than half of the drivers. Mike Wallace and Tony Stewart tapped bumpers on the backstretch. The cars were packed together so tightly that 22 other cars were caught up in the wreck. No one was seriously hurt, but many cars were damaged so badly that they couldn't challenge for the lead.

Racers drove around the track for several caution laps. When the race restarted with 14 laps to go, Earnhardt jumped out to a lead of three car lengths.

Some of the damaged cars from the wreck leaked oil onto the track. This time, officials waved the red flag. All the cars stopped with just four laps to go.

Earnhardt Jr. held off Michael Waltrip and Jeff Gordon.

When the race restarted, Earnhardt was just ahead of Michael Waltrip. Waltrip tried to find a way to get around Earnhardt. As they came around the final corner, the cars were right next to each other. Earnhardt flew over the finish line just .02 seconds ahead of Waltrip, one of the closest finishes in NASCAR history.

Earnhardt Jr. did a spinout in the infield to celebrate his victory.

Talladega Superspeedway

Talladega Superspeedway is one of the fastest, most exciting tracks in NASCAR. It's also NASCAR's longest track. Two NASCAR Cup races take place there each year, one in the spring and one in the fall.

Fans love Talladega. The races there usually include many wrecks and lead changes. Some of the closest finishes in NASCAR happen at Talladega. The track has seating for 160,000 people. For most races, thousands of extra people pay to watch the race standing up.

"I don't get nervous for very many races. I do get nervous before Talladega. I think all drivers do."
—Jeff Burton, Spring 2001, *Men and Speed*

CHAPTER 2

Track Design

Talladega Superspeedway is modeled after Daytona International Speedway. NASCAR founder Bill France Sr. built Daytona. The first NASCAR race at Daytona was in 1959. In the late 1960s, France wanted to build another track just like it.

France and his partners picked a spot between Birmingham, Alabama, and Atlanta, Georgia. France wanted people from these large cities to be able to get to the racetrack easily. The site was part of an old airport. Talladega Superspeedway opened in 1969.

Copying Daytona

As the home of the Daytona 500, Daytona is the most important racetrack in NASCAR. France gave Talladega the same design as Daytona, only slightly bigger. Talladega is 2.66 miles (4.28 kilometers) long. Daytona is 2.5 miles (4 kilometers) long.

Drivers have plenty of room to race three-wide at Talladega.

Learn about:

→ Early days of the track

→ Track layout

→ Speeds on the track

Both Daytona and Talladega are tri-ovals. The tri-oval design has two sections, or legs, on the frontstretch. It also has two big turns and a long backstretch. At Talladega, the two frontstretch legs are each 2,150 feet (655 meters) long. The flat backstretch is 4,000 feet (1,219 meters) long. The two turns are 3,750 feet (1,143 meters) long and have a high banking of 33 degrees. The frontstretch has 18 degrees of banking.

Fans cheer for the drivers at every turn.

High banking in the turns allows the cars to keep up their incredible speed.

The steep turns and long straightaways help keep speeds high. Several NASCAR speed records have been set at Talladega.

"At Talladega the banking turns the race car, and the air holds the car on the ground."
—Derrike Cope, *American Zoom*

Drivers draft to try to gain extra speed.

Speeds at Talladega are so fast that NASCAR tries to slow down the cars. NASCAR teams have to add restrictor plates to their cars' engines for racing at Talladega. Restrictor plates keep the cars from going more than about 190 miles (306 kilometers) per hour.

"When you are racing at Talladega, you know something big is going to happen."
—Ken Schrader, 10-12-00, The Auto Channel

Too Close for Comfort

The track design and restrictor plates cause cars to race together in large packs. If one driver makes a small mistake, several cars can get caught up in a wreck.

In the past few years, NASCAR officials have tried to break up the large packs of cars. They now make the race teams use smaller fuel tanks. Drivers have to take pit stops more often. More pit stops can help break up the large packs.

A Talladega wreck can take out many cars.

"I think any time you race three-wide or four-wide all day long, it is more mentally demanding. You have to pay attention and you're really on top of the steering wheel all day long."
—Ricky Rudd, 4-25-04, AP

The holes in a restrictor plate allow only a small amount of air to get to the combustion chamber.

Restrictor Plates

At both Daytona and Talladega, NASCAR makes teams use restrictor plates. A restrictor plate is a square piece of metal with four holes. The restrictor plate keeps the normal amount of air from getting into the combustion chamber.

In an engine, fuel and air are pulled into the combustion chamber. The spark plug makes a spark that creates an explosion. That explosion pushes the pistons out. The back and forth motion of the pistons powers the car.

When less air gets into the chamber, the explosion will be smaller. A smaller explosion means less power for the engine and a lower speed. NASCAR officials believe lower speeds are safer for drivers. The faster the car is racing, the less reaction time the driver has to avoid crashes.

TRACK DIAGRAM
Talladega Superspeedway

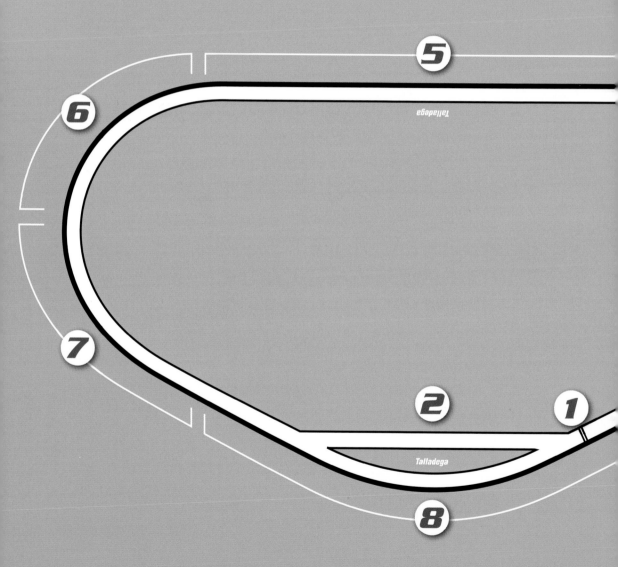

1. **Start-finish line**

2. **Pit road**

3. **Turn 1**

4. **Turn 2**

5. **Backstretch**

6. **Turn 3**

7. **Turn 4**

8. **Frontstretch**

CHAPTER 3

Race Day at Talladega

Talladega is a fan favorite. Races at Talladega usually have big wrecks, close finishes, or both.

Coming from Behind

The 2000 Winston 500 had one of the most unlikely finishes seen in NASCAR. Legendary driver Dale Earnhardt Sr. had led several times during the race. After a late pit stop, he fell to 15th place with 14 laps to go.

Earnhardt then got trapped in a large pack of cars. Nine laps later, he fell three spots to 18th place. Suddenly, with five laps to go, Earnhardt found an opening. He quickly began to pass cars. Soon, he was in fourth place. By the end of the next lap, he had passed everyone else in front of him. Earnhardt stayed in the lead and crossed the finish line first.

Dale Earnhardt Sr. made a habit of winning at Talladega.

Learn about:

→ An amazing win

→ 27-car pileup

→ Sadler's rollover

Ryan Newman had a wild wreck during the 2003 Aaron's 499.

The Big One

Drivers expect a big wreck every time they race at Talladega. They call it "the big one." The cars are so close together and going so fast, a big wreck almost cannot be avoided.

One of the biggest wrecks in NASCAR history happened at Talladega during the Aaron's 499 on April 6, 2003. Only three laps had been completed when Ryan Newman's car blew a tire. His car spun out of control. He was near the front at the time, so most of the cars were behind him. They had no place to go and couldn't see what was going on in all the smoke.

Drivers slammed on their brakes, spun out, and banged into one another. The pileup included 27 cars. Many of them were too damaged to continue the race. NASCAR had to stop the race to clean up the mess.

Spectacular Wreck

Another big wreck happened during the EA Sports 500 on September 28, 2003. Elliott Sadler was in the middle of a group of cars coming around to the frontstretch. The car behind him nudged his back bumper. The contact sent Sadler's car skidding toward the infield grass.

Elliott Sadler's #38 car rolled at Talladega in 2003.

Sadler was not hurt even after rolling over five times.

The car suddenly took off and seemed to float upside down in the air for a second. It landed on its hood and slid across the grass. When it got back up to the track, it rolled over five times. Sadler's car finally landed on its tires. The crash looked terrible, but Sadler was not seriously hurt. And surprisingly, no other cars crashed.

CHAPTER 4

Talladega's Best

Dale Earnhardt Sr. was one of the most successful drivers in Talladega's history. He won 10 Cup races there. Earnhardt had several famous wins, including the 2000 Winston 500, where he staged an amazing comeback.

His son Dale Earnhardt Jr. has already won five races at the track. He won four in a row between 2001 and 2003. His last win there was in 2004. That win brought the family total to 15 and counting.

The Allisons

Bobby Allison was one of the great drivers in NASCAR's early history. He won 84 races in his career, including four at Talladega. In 1993, he was inducted into the International Motorsports Hall of Fame, which is also in Talladega.

Dale Earnhardt Jr. is continuing his father's winning ways at Talladega.

Learn about:

→ The Earnhardts

→ The Allisons

→ Unbreakable record

Davey Allison was just beginning to dominate at Talladega before he died tragically in 1993.

Bobby's son, Davey Allison, will always be remembered at Talladega. Davey's first Cup race was at Talladega in 1985. He won his first Cup race there in 1987. He then won two more races at Talladega. In 1993, Davey Allison died after his helicopter crashed in the infield at Talladega as the pilot was trying to land.

Other Champions

Two other drivers have won four races at Talladega. Like Bobby Allison, Buddy Baker was one of the best drivers of the early days. Darrell Waltrip also won four races at Talladega in the 1970s and 1980s.

Bill Elliott had a different kind of success at Talladega. He won two races there, but he is probably best known for his qualifying runs. Elliott won the pole position at Talladega a record eight times. He also holds the NASCAR record for fastest qualifying speed. Elliott qualified at 212.809 miles (342.474 kilometers) per hour for the 1987 Winston 500. That speed is still a NASCAR record.

Restrictor plates will probably keep anyone from breaking Elliott's record at Talladega. But it's the track design that makes races exciting at Talladega Superspeedway.

Bill Elliott (#9) helped make Talladega a fast, exciting racetrack.

Glossary

backstretch (BAK-strech)—the straight part of a racetrack that is opposite the frontstretch

bank (BANGK)—the angle of the track; if a track has a high bank, the top of the track is much taller than the bottom of the track.

caution (KAW-shun)—a time during a race when drivers have to slow down and are not allowed to pass; a caution occurs after a crash, when the track crew has to clean up debris, or during bad weather.

frontstretch (FRUHNT-strech)—the part of a racetrack where the race begins and ends

infield (IN-feeld)—the area inside a racetrack, surrounded on all sides by the track

pole position (POHL puh-ZISH-uhn)—the inside spot in the front row of cars at the beginning of a race

qualifying (KWAHL-uh-fye-ing)—the timed laps drivers run before a race to earn a starting spot in the race

restrictor plate (ri-STRIKT-ur PLAYT)— a device that limits the power of a race car's engine; the restrictor plate slows the car's speed.

Read More

Cavin, Curt. *Terrific Tracks: The Coolest Places to Race.* The World of NASCAR. Maple Plain, Minn.: Tradition Books, 2004.

Johnstone, Michael. *NASCAR.* The Need for Speed. Minneapolis: LernerSports, 2002.

Schaefer, A. R. *Dale Earnhardt Jr.* NASCAR Racing. Mankato, Minn.: Capstone Press, 2005.

Woods, Bob. *Dirt Track Daredevils: The History of NASCAR.* The World of NASCAR. Excelsior, Minn.: Tradition Books, 2003.

Internet Sites

FactHound offers a safe, fun way to find Internet sites related to this book. All of the sites on FactHound have been researched by our staff.

Here's how:

1. Visit *www.facthound.com*

2. Choose your grade level.

3. Type in this book ID **0736843795** for age-appropriate sites. You may also browse subjects by clicking on letters, or by clicking on pictures and words.

4. Click on the **Fetch It** button.

FactHound will fetch the best sites for you!

Index